L[illegible]g Youth Work

Reflecting on Your Church-based Youth Ministry

Colin Bennett
Freelance Christian Trainer and Educator

GROVE BOOKS LIMITED
RIDLEY HALL RD CAMBRIDGE CB3 9HU

Contents

Acknowledgments

Thanks to all my family and friends and the staff team at Moorlands College and Godfirst Christchurch. Without you this book would not exist. As a thank you, the best gift I can give to you are the words of our Lord and Saviour Jesus Christ. 'As the Father has loved me, so have I loved you. Now remain in my love.' (John 15.9)

First Impression March 2021
ISSN 1748-3492
ISBN 978 1 78827 157 8

1 Introduction

The young youth pastor was beaming. He had run a very successful week of youth and children's ministry during the COVID-19 pandemic and was so pleased with himself as he turned to me and said, 'That has got to be the best piece of ministry ever, right?' I smiled and said that it was very good. By experience I knew that it ticked so many boxes in terms of youth work and ministry, particularly at a difficult time. But was it really *the best*?

I knew that to get an accolade like that, a piece of youth work and ministry would have to demonstrate beyond any reasonable doubt that it had met an incredibly robust and extensive set of objective criteria. It would also need to have shown eternal value from God's perspective. So here is the challenge before us, as we engage in critical evaluation of youth work and ministry.

This booklet is designed to explore the dilemmas surrounding the evaluation process. It will look at the essence of evaluation, what youth work and ministry are and what criteria they can be measured by. It will explore why evaluation is such a vital part of the professional youth work and ministry toolbox and will conclude with practical recommendations.

Evaluation is a vital part of the professional youth work toolbox

Twenty-five years ago, one of my colleagues told me that she had found Christians to be not only poor at evaluation, but also uninterested in developing any evaluation process that could examine difficult questions around the effectiveness of youth work and ministry. She suggested that it was easier and simpler to carry out a piece of work and then move on to the next task. This lack of reflection on practice was a primary reason why many youth work and ministry projects struggled to flourish. That comment has been a motivating factor in writing this booklet. My hope is that more of us would take time to think carefully about what we do and why we do it—not only in our ministry but also in our daily lives.

This booklet will explore some biblical and theoretical underpinning in regard to the importance of evaluation. It will examine frameworks and tools that can aid an evaluative process, reflect on practitioners and young people's comments and close with recommendations and conclusions.

2 The Challenge of Evaluation

In thinking about what we do, why we do it and how effective we are in youth work and ministry, it is clear that there is space for both *shallow* and *deep* reflection. It could be argued that in life we are constantly in an evaluative process. Even before getting out of bed, we might be thinking about the kind of sleep we have had, the way we are feeling, our state of mind and health, all before we even begin to think of washing (or not—especially if we are late!) and preparing ourselves for the day ahead. What shall we wear? What shall we eat? What shall we pack for the day?

This is *shallow* reflection; it is a vital part of judging and evaluating. Omit it or get it wrong, and you will regret it all day long. If you have ever had to speak to a young person who has not themselves carried out this daily reflection about their problems with body odour or oral hygiene you will understand what I mean! In contrast, *deep* reflection gets to the heart of who we are, why we are here and how we should live. It focuses on our identity, significance, purpose and personal effectiveness. It delves into how we perceive ourselves and others. It uncovers who we can trust and be secure in, and what on earth we are doing with our lives. It can lead to effective action, requiring wisdom, prayer and care. This is *deep* reflection.

As a discipline, reflection in youth work and ministry challenges us to dig deeply into our motivations, methodologies and fruitfulness. As a result, we can consider what is of value, what is true, what is measurable and what has a lasting and eternal consequence.

Frustrated youth workers can feel they are getting nowhere and assume their employers only focus on the cost of everything and the value of nothing. However, honest critical reflection can explore such notions, especially if all parties concerned are involved. Evaluation itself has deep roots in the Bible; however, it is often overlooked by many as another potential resource, and it is this notion that will now be addressed.

Thinking Biblically about Evaluation

When seeking to apply the Bible to ideas surrounding evaluation, established frameworks can be particularly useful. In my book on faith development, I introduced a theological framework called STOP (Scripture, Tradition, Own your own baggage and Penetrating the global cultures).[1] While this is a great tool to use for in-depth theological work, particularly in youth work and ministry, for the purpose of finding a biblical imperative for evaluation, Wilson's take on the five-act play—covering creation and fall, Israel and history, poets and prophets, Jesus and rescue, restoration and hope—has more merit.[2]

Evaluation and the Five-act Play

In the first act, creation and fall, God works to a clear plan in creating all things (Genesis chapters 1 to 3). *Creatio ex nihilo* means 'everything from nothing.' Evaluatively, it is masterly: all things fit. And importantly, everything was good and in perfect order. However, Genesis 3 highlights humanity's fall from God's grace and into sin. Again, things are worked out within the plan, albeit a sad one, meaning human expulsion from Eden. The vital point here is that even when things go horrifically wrong, God's planning as part of an evaluative process is flawless. It gives us much hope as we make our contingency plans.

God's planning as part of an evaluative process is flawless

Part of that plan is the second and third acts. This is the formation of the people of Israel through Noah, Abraham, Isaac, Jacob and culminating in that perfect covenant God made with Moses for the chosen people of Israel—the Ten Commandments. Here God not only codifies how *all* people are to live, but also how they can live in harmony with God and with each other by following the covenant. This ancient covenant is still the only real objective benchmark humanity has, and this notion of criteria and benchmarks will reappear later.

Perhaps unsurprisingly, the history of Israel shows that God's people cannot keep the covenant; each time they fall they cry out to God, and he sends leaders and prophets to help the people renew their commitment to this covenant. The wisdom literature and the books of the prophets display two intertwined themes: a call to reason with God (Ps 86.5; Isa 1.18), alongside a desire for a saviour to come to liberate the people from their fallen state (Ps 55.16; Isa 53). Israel is still waiting for redemption and complete reconciliation with God through the Messiah. This is all part of God's master plan—an evaluative process bound up in humanity's relationship with the creator.

Wilson completes the Christian message by introducing the two final acts. Firstly, in Jesus and rescue, we see the arrival of the long-awaited Messiah, Immanuel—God with us. From miraculous birth to signs and wonders, to atoning death, to resurrection and ascension into heaven, the plan unfolds, drawing in many to become Jesus' disciples, which continues even to this day. In the Nazareth manifesto (Luke 4.18–19), Jesus outlines his life's work, bringing healing and salvation to many; even telling of his death, resurrection and ascension before they happen (John 16). Jesus commissions his disciples to continue making disciples who are faithful to God's covenant; this is brilliantly summarized in Matt 22.36–40—namely, to love God and love your neighbour—a neat shortcut to fulfilling God's covenant (the decalogue).

The Final Act—Restoration and Hope

This is the universal church, living out the vibrant message of hope and reconciliation, true to Jesus. The Book of Acts, the Pauline epistles and other New Testament writings deal with the challenges of the fledgling church. Two thousand years later, the worldwide church is still seeking to be faithful to the commission Jesus issued. It is still seeking to become the spotless bride of Christ which will one day be reunited with God in the new heaven and the new Earth, fulfilling the eternal plan (Revelation 21). This is the perfect example of an evaluative process in action.

The task is to move from the only perfect example of planning, creating and intervening and evaluating—the greatest story ever told—to our simpler challenge, of how to ensure practically that evaluation is at the heart of youth work and youth ministry.

However, before doing this, I wish to reinforce this biblical narrative as being the benchmark for all youth workers and youth ministers. God expects every person to live holy and upright in him. However, especially for those who are influencers of young people, a high bar is set. In Matthew 18 Jesus indicates that children and young people are exemplars of greatness. Jesus said to his disciples, 'Unless you change and become like little children, you will never enter the kingdom of God. Therefore, whoever takes the lowly position of this child is the greatest in the kingdom of heaven' (Matt 18.3–4). A youth worker or minister must realize how precious the young are, and heed Jesus' subsequent warning when he continues in verse 6:

> If anyone causes one of these little ones…to stumble…it would be better for them to have a large millstone hung round their neck and to be drowned in the depths of the sea.

This warning strikes to the heart of the character and motivation of the youth worker or minister. They are *expected* to be Christ-like in character and attitude, loving God and their neighbour as they love themselves (Matt 22.36–40).

Thinking Practically about Evaluation in a Youth Work and Ministry Context

My hope is that you will now be convinced that it is vitally important for the youth worker or minister to engage with an evaluation process. Having briefly reflected on a biblical basis, it is essential for us to understand the very practical nature of evaluation. While it is something we probably all do, even unthinkingly, to determine what is truly effective professional youth workers and ministers should seek an evaluative process that is embedded into their practice framework. However, while efficiency and value for money are important, the true essence of evaluation and lasting effectiveness is found in a wise, informed and measured approach to practice.

Encouragingly, since the 1990s, youth work and ministry have flourished in churches to the point today when the church in Britain is seen as the largest employer of youth workers and youth ministers. While some churches are uncertain about investing in youth ministry, others see employing a family, youth or children's worker or minister as essential. The question raised from this is how do churches evaluate the effectiveness of this work and what benchmarks do they use when measuring?

The National Youth Agency, in line with the English and Welsh Government, developed a set of National Occupational Standards (NOS) in line with many other professions in the 1990s. The first set of standards for youth work were developed in 2002 and have since gone through a number of revisions. At the same time, a robust definition of professional youth work was formulated; it is to:

> Enable young people to develop holistically, working with them to facilitate their personal, social and educational development, to enable them to develop their voice, influence and place in society and to reach their full potential.[3]

However, there is a problem deciding on a similar professional definition of youth *ministry*; there are no NOS for Christian ministry, let alone youth ministry. While it may be assumed that youth ministry is synonymous with Christian youth work, there are differences. As helpful as the youth work definition is, it does not go far enough for the Christian minister. Helpfully, Steven Croft sees ministry as three-dimensional, focusing on three facets: diaconal, presbyterial and episcopal:

> …the first dimension is primarily a ministry of service; the second of service of the Word, and of sacraments and prayer; and the third of vision, unity, enabling, and watching over self and other.[4]

From Croft's work it can be deduced that youth ministry is any work that seeks, in a Christian sense, to serve and oversee young people, not only practically and pastorally, but also in devotional prayer, in setting vision and empowering the young person. This would generally be in the context of the individual's peer group, their community and their family.

Youth ministry would normally be delivered by a team led by someone who seeks unity in Christ, overseeing the team in a spirit of reconciliation to Jesus and each other (Matt 22.36–40). Brierley's classic work highlighting the nuances between Christian youth work and ministry still stands the test of time.[5]

Youth Work and Ministry Professional

I think this continuum helpfully highlights the tension between youth ministry and youth work:

youth ministry ———————————————— youth work

According to Brierley, the following roles would be placed along this line from left to right:

- Christian church minister or evangelist
- Youth pastor / minister
- Christian youth and community work professional
- Non-Christian youth and community work professional

Brierley's all-encompassing phrase 'youth work and ministry professional' intersects the roles listed above. In using this phrase he clearly outlines that youth ministers and youth workers should be professional and that these ministers / workers should understand the subtle nuances between all the roles identified.

He goes further by suggesting that the term 'youth work and ministry professional' is a neat way of overcoming the communication challenges faced by such workers listed above. He continues to encourage those involved in this field of study to use this phrase not only when talking to fellow believers, but also in engaging with non-Christian professionals.

It also highlights the tensions between the youth pastor and the professional Christian youth worker, with each seeking to understand their effectiveness by evaluating their own end product. However, in setting targets, having SMART goals (Specific, Measurable, Achievable, Realistic and Time-related), formulating objectives, managing findings, and enabling and empowering young people to reach their full potential, is it still possible to miss the mark? The next chapter will explore this.

Reflection

- To what extent do you agree that the Bible is vital for evaluating effectiveness in youth work or ministry? If you do not perceive it to be vital, what robust framework would you use and why?
- How useful is Brierley's phrase 'youth work and ministry professional' in describing and communicating more effectively to those outside of Christianity what a Christian youth worker is?

3 Selecting and Setting Criteria for Evaluation

To help in exploring criteria for evaluation, a narrative approach has been adopted. The following is an amalgam of real-life stories interwoven with theory and theology.

> A young youth worker (let us call them Chris*; these are anonymized amalgams and gender neutral), has just entered their first post as a youth minister in a church that has never had a full-time youth worker before. While the youth worker set their sights on getting to know the young people in the church, the youth ministry team of volunteers and the families associated with the ministry, the church leader (let us call them Sam*) and their team try to set realistic aims and outcomes for the youth ministry. So what targets should Sam and the church set for Chris?
>
> On examining Chris's job description, it is expected that the worker should engage with young people in the church and those in the community (non-Christians), and see the ministry grow not only in depth, but also numerically. Families in the church with young people should be happy with their children's spiritual growth, alongside the congregation being happy with Chris's involvement with the life of the church, and Chris taking a lead in all-age worship. Chris is expected to play an active role in the community and interact with non-Christian young people, perhaps even doing school assemblies. Alongside this, Chris is expected to recruit, develop and lead a team of volunteer youth ministers who will engage well with young people.
>
> Already, the problem emerges. Where is the evaluative process explored, explained or examined?
>
> It is not. So what happens next?
>
> Chris busies themself with their new role. Generally, they put in lots and lots of hours. Their supervisor Sam would probably in the early days keep a bit of a close eye on Chris, but after a while the initial flush of enthusiasm to do this might wane because Chris is seen as doing a good job. The church is happy, the young people seem happy, the leadership are happy. For Chris and Sam, the first year is fine. But without any realization of the need for a robust evaluative process there could be rocky times ahead.

Evaluating to Encourage

Honest evaluation is needed here. I think even the most cynical would agree that the motives behind most churches' ministries are fair and honest. But an evaluative process is vital from the outset. Here it is totally missing. It may be missing through ignorance. Or is it an anxiety about the difficulty of measuring both the evidence behind effective youth work and ministry, and the evidential basis of effective youth ministry? What evidence should be sought and measured?

How can Chris and Sam prove the effectiveness of their work without evidence?

Apart from numerical growth and the number of active groups running in the youth work, how can a leader measure whether the ministry is effective and that *they* are also effective as ministers?

For some, the notion of evidence-based evaluation can feel threatening, cold and clinical. The image of an Ofsted inspector might come to mind. In the case study, Chris and the church leader, Sam, both serve diligently. But are they effective in what they do? Are they using their time and energy wisely? Working face-to-face with people, young or old, especially in a pastoral context, can be very draining. This is indisputable, and taking time out to rest and recuperate is vital.

However, engaging with a quality evaluative process can really help the stretched worker by giving a sense of achievement. If the individual has a clear set of aims, outcomes, targets and performance indicators as part of the process of ensuring quality as evidence, it will generate a sense of accomplishment. It is easy to spend all the God-given hours in pursuit of doing a good enough job, especially for the raw recruit to youth work or ministry. Establishing criteria for the work undertaken helps to alleviate the stress and pressure associated with youth work and ministry. The exciting thing is that there are plenty of evaluative tools and frameworks which are in circulation, and these will be explored shortly.

Returning to the Narrative

So, Chris the youth worker has made a good start and Sam the church leader agrees. But shortly after—maybe 6 months or even 18 months—the honeymoon period is over. A troubled time unfolds.

Chris experiences the first signs of burnout alongside the surprise of many complaints from in and outside the church. Chris now realizes the expectation placed on the worker and becomes schooled in the juggling act of youth work and ministry. That is, listening to and engaging with the young people, their parents, the youth work team, Sam and the other church leaders, members of the congregation, the schools and the local community. Alongside this, the challenge of trying to build a private life, and the sense of friendlessness due to unsociable working hours, all contribute to an emotional meltdown for Chris. Chris realizes that one full-time worker cannot do everything and cannot be everything to everyone.

How will it all end?

What happens next depends on a number of factors. Perhaps Sam and the church leadership will support Chris and things will work out well. Or, maybe Chris will weather the storm and see it as part of the spiritual battle of leadership (Jas 1.1–2). Perhaps Chris will quit this problematic church and find another better suited? It is also possible that Chris could give up under the strain and decide ministry is not God's plan for them.

A Familiar Story?

A clear evaluative process focusing on quality assurance, targeted support and clear metrics would help clarify this youth work and ministry dilemma. Managing realistic expectations is hard enough as it is. Without a robust process that includes clear targets, milestones of achievement, steps of progress, regular routine reviews and agenda setting—in fact, quality management structures—then the chances are the youth work and ministry described will stutter and stall.

An evaluative process means a continuous loop of feedback, leading to change and correction on the way towards clearly agreed targets. It is not dissimilar to a plane in flight, which is continually correcting its path towards a known destination. It operates using navigation tools, adjusting its course using the highest form of technology, often subject to changing conditions, and uses the highest quality resources to ensure successful outcomes for all involved. The air industry is known as the safest and most effective form of travel.

Even as I write, many youth workers are on furlough due to the ravaging of the UK church in the grip of COVID-19. It has challenged the perception about the need for any full-time youth minister in a church. This booklet is a timely support in favour of youth work and ministry.

The next chapter will help examine the resources, tools and frameworks which youth workers, youth ministers and churches should consider employing in the quest for effectiveness in ministry.

Reflections

- To what extent do you identify with Chris's dilemma?
- A robust evaluative process could help both Chris and Sam. To what degree are you convinced by this?

4 Processes, Methods and Tools

Any quality management and leadership structures should draw on a selection of methods, processes and evaluative tools. In this section, some tools will be explored as an aid to those involved in Christian youth work and ministry. In contemporary society, quality feedback from customers and clients is always being sought to enhance specific products and services. However, in youth work and ministry, customer/congregation views about ministry effectiveness seem rarely sought. Perhaps this is because churches do not often seek feedback about effectiveness.

At my previous workplace, Moorlands College, student feedback is the lifeblood of progress, change and development. Colleges and universities such as Moorlands have had to undergo rigorous levels of evaluation (benchmarked by the Teaching and Excellence Framework), and feedback is especially gathered from students, using the National Student Survey, which has a credibility of its own.[6] Over the last 30 years in particular, schools have also been rigorously inspected, and are expected to record and publicize exam results, on top of the reports from Ofsted.

In my opinion, a higher level of requesting and listening to feedback—and acting on it—should be the norm in church. Perhaps there is a fear that a 'vox pop' approach might lead a church into error. However, I believe that with robust, prayerful, wise and biblically based approaches to planning, monitoring and evaluating, there is no reason to fear. In fact, it seems the very opposite is true.

So how can churches improve their approach to evaluation? By not overthinking things and making evaluation more complicated than it needs to be, and instead keeping strategies, processes, tasks and systems as simple as possible.[7]

Processes and Methods

While youth workers and ministers possibly know the 'why'—the vision behind their engagement with young people—they may be confused by the *strategies* needed to meet the vision. This is the 'what' and the 'how,' namely the processes and methods used to do the 'what' and fulfil the 'why.' This is where I have seen a breakdown in ministry.

Let us return to the narrative used in chapter three to explore this dilemma.

Chris knows the vision of the church is to make disciples who mature and multiply (the 'why' drawn from Matt 28.16–20). The church's strategy to achieve this is to use its programmes and events to disciple individuals intentionally (the 'what'). So Chris and the team contextualize this into the youth work fairly straightforwardly. It is what happens next that is the crunch.

Processes are the consistent, step-by-step structures that define the stages and milestones of a youth work team's activities. This is how Chris's team could try and achieve their aims and goals. Methods, on the other hand, are the ways and tactics used to support young people through the youth work process. This could be how Chris's team are going to achieve things in detail. For example, the youth work team might use informal educational processes, with key features, markers and stages. Chris and the team may use small group work and mentoring as common methods within this process.[8]

Having both processes and methods synchronized is crucial in running quality youth work and ministry. Knowing the 'why,' the 'what' and the 'how' surrounding a ministry, and its aim for effectiveness, is essential. If processes and methods are not linked together it is difficult to measure how things are progressing, which will hamper any form of meaningful evaluation.

One significant issue is external reference and accountability. The youth worker and youth minister often have no clear external body to hold them answerable to, such as Ofsted. Some may think this is a good thing, meaning less pressure on meeting set national standards, and the work being free from close scrutiny. Sadly, the flip side of this could mean that less effort might go into ensuring the youth work and ministry is genuinely pursuing excellence. Despite all this, external objectivity could help the stretched youth work team by having their excellent work validated. As a consequence, an opportunity is then missed for the team, the young people, the church and the local community celebrating the achievement together. I will never forget the times we at Moorlands rejoiced when we were given positive external comments. For we know that 'No discipline is pleasant at the time, but painful. Later on, however, it produces a harvest of righteousness and peace' (Heb 12.11).

Digging Deeper

A big advantage in terms of being effective in supporting young people is that youth work and ministry teams do have a natural tendency to focus on the process of genuinely caring for young people rather than simply being outcome driven. I think youth work has always been focused on how to relate to young people and their communities, rather than being worried about outcomes.[9] Tumilty suggests youth workers tend to have a natural bias towards either product or process, but I think professionally it is vital to balance both product and process. In other words, balancing what to achieve with young people (product) and how to go about doing it (process).

Quality assurance can aid this process in being: 'A system of procedures, checks, audits, and corrective actions used to ensure that...*an organization, work or a project*...meets established standards.'[10] A quality assurance culture seeks to get things right first time, making continuous evaluation in the moment rather than waiting until some end point to evaluate effectiveness.

While various methods can be employed to aid youth work and ministry, it is crucial that they are evaluated against criteria, and this is where the discussion goes next.

The Toolkit of the Reflective Evaluator

> 'The unexamined life is not worth living'—Socrates

Evaluation should include honest reflection at the outset. It is easy to deceive even ourselves. Are we doing a great job when we are not, or think we are doing a poor job when that is just not true? Anyone struggling with heightened perfectionism, imposter syndrome, overconfident arrogance bordering on rebellion—or even all three—needs sober or accurate judgment (Rom 12.3).

Honest and accurate evaluation may be more difficult than we first think. We might find ourselves engaging with emotional responses, such as fear of judgment or failure. We also might find in some job roles that if we begin to be completely honest our funding stream might come under threat, or it may even lead to us losing our job and negatively affecting our organization or church.

> I am mentally drained by constantly having to prove my youth work worth in funding applications, endlessly setting out the economic benefits and outcomes achieved. The inducement to lie, distort and exaggerate my effectiveness, because I know this will help my case, is an ever-present temptation.[11]

In contrast, a robust framework of honest evaluation embedded into our youth work and ministry *from the outset* can outweigh the negative connotations surrounding the idea of measuring achievement. So the best way to undertake any youth work and ministry should include a self-evaluation framework from the outset. Two examples of templates are included in the endnotes.[12]

Seeking agreement and engagement from all stakeholders involved is essential—church leadership, youth team, parents, youth etc—and this is often termed 360-degree feedback. Additionally, recruiting an experienced external consultant to facilitate this process might help.[13]

For this, I suggest that a benchmark of quality standards be used at the start of any new phase of youth work or ministry. Again, there are many examples of youth work standards, and during studying for my master's degree I developed a survey tool to help summarize many popular approaches. CONE (Figure 2) is an attempt to capture a quality framework that can be used. My studies allowed me to trial it in a church, and it was viewed positively by the youth work and ministry team there.

Figure 2: Overview of the CONE Survey Tool

Culture of Church and Community Engagement

The culture of a church (or organization) and its engagement with its local community will shape any youth work practice. If a church or organization is open and welcoming, then people living around it will be interested in it. If not, it is likely that they will not. This is such an obvious starting point and yet many churches and Christian organizations in the UK have somehow forgotten this simple idea. Young people respond to friendly, warm atmospheres in a positive way. This is the first step in community engagement, and therefore the first criteria. It is key.

Openness to God

Openness to God is the prerequisite of a church or Christian organization. Young people need to see that believers are really open to God and God's ways. All of us, God included, are sick of religious ways (Isaiah 58). Listening to God's word and Spirit are the essential starting points of godly women and men. Jesus' words encourage us to listen to him, the good shepherd, remain in his love, obey his commands, and be full of joy (John 10 and John 15.9–12). Openness to God is the fruit of authentic Christianity.

National Standards

If we only focus on the church or organization and local community, there is a missing component. All nations have some notion of what they expect from the future generations. They also have standards, however informal, that should govern how the older generations assist the younger ones. As previously mentioned, the National Youth Agency have developed a set of detailed criteria called the National Occupational Standards for Youth Work,[14] alongside help for evaluation.[15] These play an essential role in the CONE framework.

ENABLE

ENABLE comes from a body of research developed in the US. It started with a disappointing study in the 1980s by Wycroft and Richter, revealing that despite efforts made to work with youth, the young people's points of need were not being reached, and church-based youth ministry was, for the most part, ineffective.[16] Strommen, Jones and Rahn, shocked by this, created the work *Youth Ministry that Transforms*. Their research suggested that youth ministry could develop professionally by using the ENABLE framework: *E*stablish personal vision; *N*urture teenage faith; *A*ccommodate developmental realities; *B*uild meaningful support; *L*ocate effectiveness indicators; *E*xpand ministry partnerships.[17] Its sound research base suggests that ENABLE is a model that is transferable across cultural contexts.

CONE Aims to Establish an Initial Benchmark

This simple CONE survey is based on a four-point Likert scale, and should be answered by the young people.

What is your church's (or organization's) youth work and ministry like?

Please grade the youth work and ministry by marking the following 20 statements with either: Strongly Agree, Agree, Disagree or Strongly Disagree.

C Culture—how your church fits with the local community

1 My church fits well in the local community.

2 My church is liked by the local community.

3 My church is friendly to all people.

4 The youth ministry team and church leaders are encouraging to all.

5 The church leaders and youth work team work together well at valuing young people and their local community.

O Openness to God

1 The people in my church know God.

2 The youth ministers in my church are trustworthy.

3 I trust this church to care for me as Jesus did for his disciples.

4 This church follows God and is on a good mission.

5 If things get tough, I know the youth team will pray and care for me.

N National standards for youth work

1 The youth team help us and care for us.

2 The youth team make good things happen with and for the young people.

3 The youth team value us as people, no matter who we are.

4 The youth work is organized, well planned and makes a difference to us.

5 The youth work fits well into the life of the local church and local community.

E ENABLED—the extent to which we are all enabled by the youth work

1 The youth team know what they are doing in leading me.

2 The youth work team knows the Bible and teaches it to me well.

3 The youth work team helps me grow as a Christian—they know what it is like for me to grow up in my family and school today.

4 The youth work team helps me grow and develop as a person—I know my life has purpose and I am secure in God's love, no matter what!

5 The youth work in this church connects very well to many different types of individuals and groups.

In essence, evaluation is a process, not an end point. It requires effort to ensure that youth work and ministry are continually being improved and challenged to change by measuring levels of effectiveness in all aspects.

Returning to the Narrative

Despite reading this far, you may still think and feel youth work and ministry is just too intangible, and that it is impossible to measure the lasting impact of youth work accurately. However, funders and employers do want to know if youth work and ministry is value for money. How might you answer those wanting to discuss this further?[18]

> Chris, the youth worker, simply feels that it is impossible really to capture objectively what goes on when a youth group meets. Chris thinks it is possible to record what the young people do and say and what part they play, but the complex interrelationships between the youth work team and young people, and the advice, guidance, counsel, mentoring and coaching that goes on week by week, are too difficult to capture objectively. Chris and Sam debate the notion, 'How can you measure the immeasurable?'

This is at the heart of informal education in youth work and ministry, especially when considering detached youth work and/or community engagement. Unlike in formal education, there are no Standard Assessment Tests (SATs) to record, no end-of-course exams to prove that effective teaching has occurred, and no college applications to complete the process.

> The church leader, Sam, identifies with this, as it is also difficult to measure the spiritual growth of a congregation. However, Sam realizes it is not enough to say we cannot measure the so-called immeasurable. Sam admits that in church there is room for not always knowing the outcome of some interventions and this is generally accepted, as long as it is possible to justify the 'what' and 'why' even if the final outcome is uncertain. Sam suggests the idea that sometimes when evaluation turns out negatively, instead of simply viewing it as failure, it might challenge individuals to dig more deeply into what can be learned from the negative responses. Sam's experiences here are invaluable, and Sam speaks at length about learning and growing most from challenges, suffering and pain. Sam shares about the dilemma of unanswered prayer as a classic example of this seeming failure. Sam has also discovered material on the idea of evidence-based practice and impact measurement, and lots of tools to help measure, record and explore effectiveness. Chris is looking forward to a new start where evaluation takes its proper place.

This help for the youth worker and minister has arisen around the notion of evidence-based practice and, in particular, the excellent contribution the Centre for Youth Impact has made, by cascading quality tools, methods and processes to the field.[19] The Brathay Trust has certainly made evaluative tools great fun to work with and no youth worker or minister should miss out on their compendium of tools and resources.[20] Likewise, thanks go to Nigel Pimlott who has published a number of key resources on youth work and ministry evaluation that have made a positive and significant impact.[21]

Final Thoughts and Issues in Developing Evaluative Processes

In looking at effective youth work and ministry, it is vital that those involved understand what the work is trying to achieve, and what it is matched against. While the two roles of youth worker and youth minister may differ to some extent, the key is that all involved should agree aims and goals and thus manage expectations.

The youth worker or minister may become the buffer between the young people and the targets set. While the employer pays the wages and sets these targets, the youth worker as a professional may be asked to undertake tasks which do not comply with good practice or even national standards. The youth worker may begin to do the work, but in time start to realize that their integrity is at risk of being compromised—or perhaps, worse still, they feel that they are not following the leading of God.

While a youth work or ministry post may evolve and shape to fit the worker rather than stick to its intended expectations, there will always come the day when the youth worker or minister leaves the post. The challenge for the church or organization is to ensure that what is left behind is in the shape that those with oversight of the work want it to be. Quality evaluation processes protect not only the worker but also the church or organization by enabling each party to follow the path God had laid out. By following clear processes, the emerging fruit can be viewed every step of the way. Just like the diligent orchard farmer who checks and evaluates the fruit regularly, the evaluation process should be both formative and summative, for as Jesus said, 'By their fruit you will know them' (Matt 7.20).

5 Reflections from Practice and Final Recommendations

No work on this topic would be complete without listening to the voice of youth workers, youth ministers and young people. I have gathered comments from six Moorlands College students or graduates who work with young people across the sector. I asked them five questions, and then asked them to gather feedback from the young people they work with about how effective their youth work and ministry is. (Anonymity of the individuals, churches and organizations and young people is protected.)

Feedback on Evaluation Challenge

1 How do you feel about the notion of your youth work and ministry being evaluated?

Person A: My initial feeling, I suppose, is one of dread. But obviously these attitudes are wrong and counterproductive. Experience has taught me that good, biblical evaluation is life-giving; it is something that we should do and do well.

Person B: I believe it is important to evaluate and review how youth work is being outworked. I am very concerned that this should not be based on numbers. It should be evaluated in terms of depth in relationship with one another and with God.

Person C: It is a great idea. Helps to show what we are doing well and areas of improvement.

Person D: It's like someone looking over your shoulder, which is never a nice feeling. An evaluation exists to improve the ministry and to learn from others and should always be done with a kind and understanding heart.

Person E: I think it's incredibly important. Anything that we value should be evaluated regularly to make sure that it is operating as best it can and fulfilling its purpose and vision.

Person F: I think that it would be a great idea.

2 How is your youth work evaluated at present?

Person A: I work under a line manager who is also an elder at the church I work for. I have subjected myself to a process where I write up a record each week (first thing I do on the first day of each week) and currently I draw out one lesson / reflection from the week gone by, which is usually something I can put into action straight away. Behind that, we have agreed more longer-term aims / goals, which I hope to make progress towards bit by bit.

Person B: In my particular small group, throughout lockdown I evaluated their engagement. For example, we did an eight-week course on prayer. A few of them really responded by showing me that in subsequent weeks they had put it into action between us meeting online. For others, they found it more difficult watching a video and then discussing it online. I evaluated this method and changed it at times in order to aid their learning approaches. One of my goals with them was to pray out loud by the end of the course. Not only did they do that, but one young person prayed out loud during a whole-church Zoom call.

Person C: The young people complete evaluation questionnaires every 6 months.

Person D: We as the leaders meet every two weeks and evaluate what we have been doing, while also trying to plan ahead. Additionally, the pastor is informed every week, but not in great detail, unless concerns or issues have been raised.

Person E: Not at all really. We often get told how great we're doing but despite our invitations, the church leadership has never sat in on our ministry or communicated clear goals and aims.

Person F: In my church I have a line-manager meeting once every 6 weeks or so but there is not much mention of the youth work; it's more on how I am.

3 What evidence is there to show your youth work and ministry is effective?

Person A: I really don't know! After serving as a student for four years, there was very little that was tangible, little that went beyond 'good relationships, good conversations, good encounters…' However, six months after leaving that place, the church ran an *Alpha* course. Five people I had been reaching attended and they brought one or two others with them who were not known to me personally. This has given me a benchmark for my ministry today.

Person B: That they show up every week no matter what their circumstances are. That, for me, speaks volumes as it shows that they are committed to a community of belonging and to deepen their faith.

Person C: The ever-increasing numbers of people attending and testimonies from both parents and the young people.

Person D: It depends how one measures, I guess. If it is all about the numbers, then we might not be classed as effective. There was not a youth group four years ago. But I would say, if one wants to find out how effective our youth group is, then they should ask our young people.

Person E: Numerical growth is a big factor for those outside of our ministry; however, internally we would also include things like baptisms, commitments. For the most part, though, we work out our effectiveness through qualitative data that we gather through our relationships with the young people on how they are growing.

Person F: It feels like it's just the amount of young people I have. But to show evidence for it, quite difficult.

4 To what extent do the church, congregation and young people evaluate your youth work and ministry?

Person A: I don't really know. I find that people don't really know how to ask this question—and they don't really know what kind of an answer to expect.

Person B: I am not sure!

Person C: They evaluate the activities and their content, the congregation complete evaluation questionnaires yearly.

Person D: The church through the pastor, as well as through ministry leaders' meetings. In those meetings (which are held maybe four times a year), we report how our ministries are doing and people have the chance to ask questions. We do try to ask the young people from time to time, but they do not seem that bothered yet.

Person E: For church and congregation, it's very little. The young people have far more of a say and we have under-18s who act as leaders and regularly provide feedback from their perspective on what we do.

Person F: I feel that as a church they do not evaluate it. I feel that we are left to it and we have to make the decisions if something is not working effectively.

5 How do you evaluate yourself in terms of life and ministry?

Person A: I have put considerable thought into this. In the end, my focus is simply on spending some time with God each morning in his word and in prayer.

Person B: I generally set goals for myself that are specific and attainable. These really help me and can ensure that I have vision and purpose. I review these goals every term and can adapt if necessary.

Person C: I write a quarterly report to the senior pastor highlighting the achievements and areas of improvement. I hold monthly meetings with family to discuss important matters.

Person D: I have two mentors, as well as a supervisor. I talk to my mentors once a month, while I talk to my supervisor weekly. Through those conversations, I am able to evaluate my own life and to be encouraged to keep on going (and to change things if necessary). And in a way, one does evaluate oneself all the time.

Person E: I use a mentor from outside my church and other friends in similar ministry who I regularly discuss and reflect with. As a team we debrief and reflect on everything we deliver and have termly vision and training evenings. We use tools such as the SWOT analysis and Kolb's Learning Cycles.

Person F: I spend time with people around, talking and praying over the ministry. Looking at what is working and what is going on in the local area but to be very honest I would say I do not spend enough time evaluating myself.

Young People's Responses about Youth Ministry Effectiveness

Context 1: I think it is effective because I feel the youth work at church is current and the leaders have spent time planning the sessions out and they know us as individuals and not as a number.

Context 2: I think it is very good. I would've found it dull if it weren't for the youth meetings. The examples and messages that come from the youth leaders are good.

Recommendations

Having set outcomes or a profit element inevitably focuses any kind of youth service on achieving targets, and risks depleting the potential for spontaneous conversations and processes. My hope is that we can rediscover what it means to do informal education and undertake this in Christian youth work, youth ministry and discipleship settings.[22]

- It can be seen from the above snapshot from students and graduates that they are craving help with evaluation. It is the responsibility of the church or organization to ensure every youth work and youth ministry post should be based on a clearly thought-out professional basis *from the outset*. The person's job description should outline the vision, mission and values of the church or organization, alongside the process of engaging with young people. This means: what the worker should consider when planning (informal structures); how the programmes and activities should be framed (outcomes set in context); how the work will be evaluated (setting criteria); and how this will all fit into the big picture of God's kingdom of peace and justice on Earth.
- When a youth work or youth minister is appointed, they should be clearly inducted into what is laid out in the point above. Regular reviews should embed this impact and evaluative process into the youth work or ministry. If the church or organization does not have the skills or expertise for this, they should have someone trained, or recruit an external person to assist in this process. This will be particularly important when things get tricky, conflicts arise and people move on. The work and ministry with firm foundations should be able to stand firm.
- The teams should pray for the wisdom of God to pervade all aspects of the work and ministry. Theories of change abound, and the work will adapt and morph as the culture changes. However, the gospel never does, and the love and grace of God is needed in every aspect of the challenges encountered. God's mission will always seek excellence and effectiveness. My prayer is that this work will spur you on to a greater quality of engagement.

Final Reflections

Evaluating effectiveness is a demanding yet essential task. Effective ministry, and in particular youth ministry, is needed if it is to be the asset to the future Christian church that this study has suggested it can be.

While Covey suggests that effectiveness is the engendering of a 'beautiful culture,' my hope is that this study will encourage churches and Christian organizations to develop a beautiful youth work and ministry culture and so change the face of present youth ministry in the UK, aided by the CONE framework.[23]

If these modest hopes are realized, then the future of the UK church may look better than some gloomy predictions, namely decline and disinterest 'unparalleled since St Augustine's visit in AD 597.'[24]

Instead, there may yet be a generation of youth workers, youth ministers and young people who will have a godly impact on our churches, communities and society, all for the glory of God.

E-val-U-ate

Can it put you straight?
You need a break
For heaven's sake!
Youth work and ministry
Tough to take
Burnt out life
Pressure, strife!
Is there no other way?
Jesus says easy yoke
Light burden
Is that a joke?
Pardon?

So, keep it simple
For all our sakes
Don't overreach
Just reach and teach?
Make disciples
One at a time
Then check it out
Might work sublime?
By the fruit you will know
If you're effective as you go.
So, evaluation is an aid not a curse
Not doing it—something far worse
Now you are an ev-al-U-ator
Live it now—not sometime later
For heaven's sake!

Notes

1 C Bennett, *Growing Upwards: The Faith Journey of Christian Young People* (Grove Youth booklet Y44) p 15.

2 A Wilson, *God*Stories: Explorations in the Gospel of God* (Eastbourne: David C Cook, 2009) chapters 1–3.

3 http://www.nya.org.uk/wp-content/uploads/2014/06/National-Occupation-Standards-for-Youth-Work.pdf (accessed on 31 March 2021).

4 S Croft, *Ministry in Three Dimensions* (London: Darton, Longman and Todd, 1999) p 40.

5 D Brierley, *Youth Ministry Theory and Practice* (Carlisle: Authentic Lifestyle, 2003) pp 25–26.

6 For TEF and NSS guidelines see https://www.officeforstudents.org.uk/advice-and-guidance/teaching/tef-data (accessed on 31 March 2021).

7 M D Watson, https://blog.processology.net/the-difference-between-strategy-process-task-and-system (accessed on 31 March 2021).

8 J Ord, *Youth Work Process, Product and Practice: Creating an Authentic Curriculum in Work with Young People* (Lyme Regis: RHP 2007) chapter 1.

9 R Tumilty, www.youthandchildrens.work/Youth-Work/Read/Youthwork-blog/Should-youth-work-have-set-outcomes-or-is-it-all-about-the-process (accessed on 31 March 2021).

10 N Pimlott and D Wiles, *Getting it Right* (Nottingham: Frontier Youth Trust, 2006).

11 N Pimlott, *Embracing the Passion* (London: SCM, 2015) p 76

12 https://learning.southdowns.gov.uk/wp-content/uploads/sites/2/2015/10/Evaluation-Toolkit.pdf (accessed on 31 March 2021)

13 https://christiancoachandmentornetwork.org.uk (accessed on 13 October 2020).

14 http://www.nya.org.uk/wp-content/uploads/2014/06/National-Occupation-Standards-for-Youth-Work.pdf (accessed 13 October 2020).

15 NYA toolkit: https://www.nya.org.uk/wp-content/uploads/2018/02/Capturing-the-Evidence.pdf (accessed 13 October 2020).

16 C Wycroff and D Richter, cited in M Strommen, K Jones and D Rahn, *Youth Ministry that Transforms* (Grand Rapids, MI: Zondervan, 2001) p 145.

17 M Strommen, K Jones and D Rahn, *Youth Ministry that Transforms* (Grand Rapids, MI: Zondervan, 2001) p 131.

18 S Gallagher, and T Morgan, 'The Process is the Product: Is There a Need for Measurement in Youth Work?' *The Journal of Youth Work* 2013, Issue 11, pp 41–65.

19 Youth Impact: https://www.youthimpact.uk/what-we-do.html (accessed 13 October 2020).

20 Youth Impact for Beginners: https://www.youthimpact.uk/impact-measurement-for-beginners/brathay-research-hub-evaluation-toolkit (accessed 13 October 2020).

21 N Pimlott: http://www.fyt.org.uk/v2/wp-content/uploads/evaluation-an-uninvited-guest-full.pdf (accessed 13 October 2020).

22 N Pimlott, *Embracing the Passion* (London: SCM, 2015) p 156.

23 S Covey, *The 7 Habits of Highly Effective Families* (London: Simon and Schuster, 1997) p 20.

24 P Brierley, *The Tide is Running Out* (Tunbridge Wells: Christian Research, 2000) p 99.